Energy and Motivation

HBR EMOTIONAL INTELLIGENCE SERIES

Harvard Business Review Press

Boston, Massachusetts

Library of Congress Cataloging-in-Publication Data

Names: Harvard Business Review Press, issuing body.
Title: Energy and motivation / Harvard Business Review.
Other titles: HBR emotional intelligence series.
Description: Boston, Massachusetts : Harvard Business Review Press,
   [2022] | Series: HBR emotional intelligence series | Includes index.
Identifiers: LCCN 2022005898 (print) | LCCN 2022005899 (ebook) |
   ISBN 9781647824365 (paperback) | ISBN 9781647824372 (epub)
Subjects: LCSH: Employee motivation. | Psychology, Industrial. | Engagement
   (Philosophy) | Vitality.
Classification: LCC HF5549.5.M63 H37 2022 (print) | LCC HF5549.5.M63
   (ebook) | DDC 658.3/14--dc23/eng/20220524
LC record available at https://lccn.loc.gov/2022005898
LC ebook record available at https://lccn.loc.gov/2022005899

Contents

Contents

Contents

Contents

Energy and Motivation

HBR EMOTIONAL INTELLIGENCE SERIES

1

The Power of Progress

An interview with Teresa Amabile
by Sarah Green Carmichael

T eresa Amabile, Harvard Business School professor and a coauthor of *The Progress Principle*, explains the importance of small wins at work in this edited interview with HBR's Sarah Green Carmichael.

Sarah Green Carmichael: *What is the progress principle?*

Teresa Amabile: It's the surprising impact of simply making forward movement on meaningful work, on the people who are doing the work. My coauthor, Steven Kramer, and I studied nearly 12,000 daily diaries of people working on creative project teams to look at their inner work life. *Inner work life* is our term for the perceptions, emotions, and motivations that people experience as they react to and make sense of the events in their workday.

What we found was that when people's inner work lives were more positive, they performed better. We asked ourselves, if inner work life has such an impact on performance, what leads to good inner work life? We found that, of all the things that can drive people in their work and make them feel good about it, the single most important is simply making progress on work that they find meaningful. That's the progress principle.

That sounds simple, but I think we've all had days when we felt like we weren't making much progress. So how much progress do you really need to make to get that feeling?

Surprisingly little. We call this the power of small wins. For example, a computer programmer was trying to track down a bug in a program, and simply solving that little problem led to an extraordinarily positive inner work life that day. Tackling that bug yielded great emotions, very powerful motivation, and positive perceptions of the work environment. Fixing a bug is a seemingly small thing. But we found that 28% of really minor—seemingly trivial—events had a strong impact on people's inner work lives in the positive direction and, unfortunately, in the negative direction, too.

What happens when that negative direction takes hold?

Unfortunately, with all kinds of work events, negative is stronger than positive. The negative inner work life impact of having a setback, for example, is two to three times stronger than the positive impact of making progress. So it's particularly important to avoid the minor hassles that can derail people's work during the average workday.

If you'd like to harness the power of these small wins and hopefully avoid some of the hassles, and you'd like to feel like you're making more progress, what should you do?

There's a lot that people can do for themselves to try to harness the progress principle. The most important is to focus. Many people in organizations are under a lot of time pressure, feeling high workload pressure. It's really easy to slip into being on a treadmill. That's our term for running all the time, feeling like you're juggling a lot of balls that are thrown at you, but not making real progress on the important work that's really going to use your creative brain, and that the organization really needs to become the innovative leader in its field.

Each of us should try to preserve at least 30 to 60 minutes a day when we're not going to be distracted by other demands, when we can really focus on the work that's most meaningful to us and most important to the organization. Sometimes that means you have to come in a half hour before anyone else or stay a half hour later. Sometimes you need to go to a coffee shop or find an unused conference room, just to get that focus.

The other thing you can do is keep track of your small wins each day. That can be very motivational.

TERESA AMABILE is a Baker Foundation Professor at Harvard Business School. Her current research program focuses on psychological and social aspects of the retirement transition. SARAH GREEN CARMICHAEL is an editor and columnist at Bloomberg Opinion and a former executive editor at *Harvard Business Review*. Follow her on Twitter @skgreen.

Adapted from "The Power of Progress," on hbr.org, August 9, 2011.

2

Managing the Hidden Stress of Emotional Labor

By Susan David

part from *Sesame Street*'s Oscar the Grouch, very few of us have the luxury of being able to be completely and utterly ourselves all the time at work. The rest of us are called upon to perform what psychologists call "emotional labor"—the effort it takes to keep your professional game face on when what you're doing is not concordant with how you feel. We do this outside the office too (making polite chitchat in the elevator when you're feeling tired and surly comes to mind), but it is perhaps more important at work because most of us are there many hours per week, and our professional images and livelihoods depend on it.

For example, your boss makes a meant-to-be inspiring comment about doing more with less, and you smile and nod, but what you'd like to do is upend the conference table. A customer talks down to you about the poor service she says she received, and you're unfailingly polite and solicitous, even though you resent being patronized. Or perhaps you simply had a poor night's sleep, yet you push yourself to remain energetic and upbeat because you've been told—more often than you care to count—that "great" leaders bring positivity and inspiration to their team.

Emotional labor is a near universal part of every job, and of life; often it's just called being polite. However, the extent to which one acts makes a meaningful difference. A person can "deep act" in a way that is still connected with their core values and beliefs at work ("Yes, the customer is being patronizing, but I empathize with her and care about solving her problem") or "surface act" ("I'll be nice here, but deep down I'm really spitting nails").

Research shows that the tendency to engage in this latter aspect of emotional labor—surface acting, in which there is a high level of incongruity between what people feel and what they show, through either faking or suppressing their emotions—comes with real costs to the person and the organization. When people habitually evoke the stress of surface acting, they'll be more prone to depression and anxiety, decreased job performance, and burnout. This has an effect on others, too: Leaders who surface act at work are more likely to be abusive to their employees, by belittling them and invading their privacy, for example. And job stress can spill over into home life. In one study of hotel employees who did a lot of surface acting on the job ("Yes, ma'am, I'd be delighted to bring you a fluffier robe!"), their spouses were more likely to see their partners' work as a source of conflict and to wish they would find another job, in the hopes that their relationship would be less strained.[1]

There are common contexts in which surface acting comes about, including:

- A mismatch between your personality (for example, level of introversion or extroversion) and what is expected from you in your role

- A misalignment of values, when what you're being asked to do doesn't accord with what you believe in

- A workplace culture in which particular ways of expressing emotion (what psychologists call "display rules") are endorsed—or not

The ideal, of course, would be to work in a job to which you are so well suited that your actions and feelings are always in perfect harmony, eliminating the need for you to be exhaustingly inauthentic all day. In real life, however, the goal of keeping your surface acting to a minimum and instead engaging in deep acting, where the role is aligned with who you truly are, is a more attainable one. Assuming you find meaning in the work you do and don't feel you're in the entirely wrong field, here are some things you can do at work to reduce your emotional labor and feel better about the way you're spending your days.

Remind yourself why you're in the job you're in

Connecting to your larger purpose—you are learning skills that are critical to your overall career; you're in a dull but stable job right now because your children need health insurance and being a good parent is important to you—will help you feel more connected to your work.

Explore "want to" thinking

It's easy to fall into a "time to make the donuts" mentality, thinking of all work as something you "have to" do. And most of us don't have the financial resources for work to truly be optional. But allowing yourself to appreciate the aspects of your job that give you a charge—maybe it's brainstorming with colleagues or making systems more efficient—elevates your work into something you choose to do, rather than something required of you. To be clear, I am not suggesting you "just think positive" or try to rationalize away real concerns. But do become more aware of the subtle traps of language in which work tasks, even ones you might enjoy, are framed as chores. If you can't find a true "want to" in key components of your work, it may be a sign that change is in order.

Do some job crafting

Consider whether you can work with your manager to tweak your job so that it's more aligned with what is of value to you. For example, if, when you visit the satellite offices of your firm, you're stimulated by the new people you meet and their different ways of doing things, perhaps you could propose a project that could involve more of these kinds of visits. The goal is to make your job more interesting so that less emotional labor is required.

When we typically think of stress at work, we focus on time pressures, information overload, and change as the causes. Yet the emotional labor that you invest in your job can be a significant source of demand and is worth considering and managing.

SUSAN DAVID is a founder of the Harvard/McLean Institute of Coaching, is on the faculty at Harvard Medical School, and is recognized as one of the world's leading management thinkers. She is the author of the number one *Wall Street Journal* bestseller *Emotional Agility*. An in-demand speaker and adviser, David has worked with the senior leadership of hundreds of major organizations, including the United Nations, Ernst & Young, and the World Economic Forum.

Note

1. Morgan A. Krannitz et al., "Workplace Surface Acting and Marital Partner Discontent: Anxiety and Exhaustion Spillover Mechanisms," *Journal of Occupational Health Psychology* 20, no. 3 (2015): 314–325.

Adapted from content posted on hbr.org, September 8, 2016 (product #H034C1).

3

How to Make Yourself Work When You Just Don't Want To

By Heidi Grant

There's that project you've left on the back burner—the one with the deadline that's growing uncomfortably near. And there's the client whose phone call you really should return—the one who does nothing but complain and eat up your valuable time. Wait, weren't you going to try to go to the gym more often this year?

Can you imagine how much less guilt, stress, and frustration you would feel if you could somehow just make yourself do the things you don't want to do when you are actually supposed to do them? Not to mention how much happier and more effective you would be?

The good news (and it's very good news) is that you can get better about not putting things off if you use the right strategy. Figuring out which strategy to use depends on why you are procrastinating in the first place. Here are some of the most likely reasons.

Reason #1: You are putting something off because you are afraid you'll screw it up.

Solution: Adopt a "prevention focus."

There are two ways to look at any task. You can do something because you see it as a way to end up better off than you are now—as an achievement or accomplishment. As in, "If I complete this project successfully I will impress my boss," or "If I work out regularly, I will look amazing." Psychologists call this a **promotion focus,** and research shows that when you have one, you are motivated by the thought of making gains, and you work best when you feel eager and optimistic. Sounds good, doesn't it? Well, if you are afraid you will screw up on the task in question, this is *not* the focus type for you. Anxiety and doubt undermine promotion motivation, leaving you less likely to take any action at all.

What you need is a way of looking at what you need to do that *isn't* undermined by doubt but rather, ideally, thrives on it. When you have a **prevention focus**, instead of thinking about how you can end up better off, you see the task as a way to hang on to what you already have—to avoid loss. For the prevention focused, successfully completing a project is a way to keep your boss from being angry or thinking less of you. Working out regularly is a way to not "let yourself go." Decades of research, which I describe in my book *Focus*, shows that prevention motivation is actually enhanced by anxiety about what might go wrong. When you are focused on avoiding loss, it becomes clear that the only way to get out of danger is to take immediate action. The more worried you are, the faster you are out of the gate.

I know this doesn't sound like a barrel of laughs, particularly if you are usually more the promotion-minded type, but there is probably no better way to get over your anxiety about screwing up than to give some serious thought to all the dire consequences of doing nothing at all. So go on, scare the pants off yourself. It feels awful, but it works.

Reason #2: You are putting something off because you don't feel like doing it.

Solution: Make like Spock and ignore your feelings. They're getting in your way.

In his excellent book *The Antidote: Happiness for People Who Can't Stand Positive Thinking*, Oliver

Burkeman points out that often when we say things like "I just can't get out of bed early in the morning," or "I just can't get myself to exercise," what we really mean is that we can't get ourselves to *feel* like doing these things. After all, no one is tying you to your bed every morning. Intimidating bouncers aren't blocking the entrance to your gym. Physically, nothing is stopping you; you just don't feel like it. But as Burkeman asks, "Who says you need to wait until you 'feel like' doing something in order to start doing it?"

Think about that for a minute, because it's really important. Somewhere along the way, we've all bought into the idea—without consciously realizing it—that to be motivated and effective we need to *feel* like we want to take action. We need to be eager to do so. I really don't know why we believe this, because it is 100% nonsense. Yes, on some level you need to be committed to what you are doing—you need to want to see the project finished, or get healthier, or get an earlier start to your day. But you don't need to *feel like doing it.*

In fact, as Burkeman points out, many of the most prolific artists, writers, and innovators have become successful in part because of their reliance on work routines that forced them to put in a certain number of hours a day, no matter how uninspired (or, in many instances, hungover) they might have felt. Burkeman reminds us of renowned artist Chuck Close's observation that "Inspiration is for amateurs. The rest of us just show up and get to work."

So if you're sitting there, putting something off because you don't feel like doing it, remember that you don't actually *need* to feel like it. There is nothing stopping you.

Reason #3: You are putting something off because it's hard, boring, or otherwise unpleasant.

Solution: Use if-then planning.

Too often, we try to solve this particular problem with sheer will: *Next time, I will* make *myself start working on this sooner.* Of course, if we actually had the willpower to do that, we would never put it off in the first place. Studies show that people routinely overestimate their capacity for self-control and rely on it too often to keep them out of hot water.

Do yourself a favor and embrace the fact that your willpower is limited. Your will may not always be up to the challenge of getting you to do things you find difficult, tedious, or otherwise awful. Instead, use **if-then planning** to get the job done.

Making an if-then plan is more than just deciding what specific steps you need to take to complete a project: It's also deciding where and when you will take those steps. For example:

> *If it is 2 p.m.,* **then** *I will stop what I'm doing and start work on the report Bob asked for.* **If** *my boss doesn't mention my request for a raise at our meeting,* **then** *I will bring it up again before the meeting ends.*

By deciding in advance *exactly* what you're going to do—and when and where you're going to do it—there's no deliberating when the time comes. There's no *Do I really have to do this now?* Or *Can this wait till later?* Or *Maybe I should do something else instead.* It's when we deliberate that willpower becomes necessary to make the tough choice. If-then plans dramatically reduce the demands placed on your willpower by ensuring that you've made the right decision way ahead of the critical moment. In fact, if-then planning has been shown in more than 200 studies to increase rates of goal attainment and productivity by 200% to 300% on average.

I realize that the three strategies I'm offering you—thinking about the consequences of failure, ignoring your feelings, and engaging in detailed planning—don't sound as fun as advice like "Follow your passion!" or "Stay positive!" But they have the decided advantage of actually being *effective*—which, as it happens, is exactly what you'll be if you use them.

HEIDI GRANT is a social psychologist who researches, writes, and speaks about the science of motivation. She is the director of learning research and development for EY Americas. Her most recent book is *Reinforcements: How to Get People to Help You* (Harvard Business Review Press, 2018). She's also the author of *Nine Things Successful People Do Differently* (Harvard Business Review Press, 2012) and *No One Understands You and What to Do About It* (Harvard Business Review Press, 2015).

Reprinted from hbr.org, originally published February 14, 2014 (product #H00OF8).

4

Four Ways to Manage Your Energy More Effectively

By Elizabeth Grace Saunders

Almost anyone can muster enough gumption for a short burst of high-energy effort. Maybe it's making a shining impression your first few weeks on a job, hitting the gym with fervor at the start of January, or spending a weekend on a remodeling project exhibiting all the peppiness of an HGTV star.

But what about after that initial burst? Do you still feel the same a few months or even a year into your new job, goal, or project? Have you abandoned your ambitions? Do you continue to push on while fighting signs of fatigue or burnout? Or do you wildly vacillate between hyperproductivity and getting nothing done?

The key to success at work and in life isn't really starting strong; it's staying strong. And one of the keys to having that staying power is the idea of self-regulation. This entails operating within lower and upper boundaries of activity by predetermining the minimum and maximum amount of action you will take toward a specific goal within a certain span of time (such as a day or a week). This keeps you from getting derailed because you dropped off or lost interest, or overdoing it and finding yourself too exhausted to continue.

As a time management coach, I've seen that there are four steps to creating this staying power. When you follow these steps, you'll be surprised to find that you'll accomplish more of your goals with less effort—and give yourself drive that lasts.

Set Upper and Lower Boundaries

The idea of goal setting is popular, especially at the start of the year. But not many individuals take the time to write out the steps that they will take to achieve their goals. And in my estimation, many fewer take the time to define their daily upper and lower boundaries for each of their goals.

In Greg McKeown's book *Effortless*, he suggests the idea of making concrete boundaries for both how little and how much you will do in a given day on your important priorities—for instance, for hitting sales numbers, you may determine to never make fewer than five sales calls in a day and never more than 10 sales calls in a day.

You can extend this into any project or goal that you want to accomplish. For example, if you want to author a book, you might decide to write no less than 30 minutes per day and no more than three hours per day to avoid burning out. Or for exercise, you may decide to work out no less than three times per week and no more than five times per week, so you get a sufficient workout in and also have time for your other priorities like spending time with your family or personal tasks. (For more on investing your time and energy, see the sidebar "Invest Your Energy.")

These boundaries give you some wiggle room but also give you the ability to stay on track over time. When you're setting your own upper and lower limits, think through what's the least you could do in a particular area to feel like you are keeping up your momentum. The goal on the low end is to not feel like you "stopped" and need to exert extra effort to break the inertia and restart. And when you're defining your upper limits, think about where you need to limit yourself so that your investment in this particular area doesn't take so much of your time that other areas of your life suffer.

INVEST YOUR ENERGY

By Peter Bregman

We all know what it takes to build and maintain our energy: sleep well, eat right, exercise, and so on. But how often do you think about how strategically you use the energy you have?

The answer for me: not very.

When I'm in a conversation, I almost always share my thoughts. In fact, if I am *near* a conversation, I often share my thoughts. I involve myself in decisions that others could make just as well or better. And when I *am* making decisions, I often delay them, struggling to make them perfect even when there are no right answers.

Those are just my *visible* energy-spending patterns. There's a whole category of *invisible* ones that sap my energy even more, such as holding on to frustrations and hurts well past their due date and

(continued)

INVEST YOUR ENERGY

worrying about the outcome of things over which I have no control.

Once I started to pay attention, I began to see how carelessly—how indiscriminately—I spend my energy.

When I *invest* my energy, I spend it writing, listening, strategizing, teaching, thinking, planning, offering my opinion selectively and with an outcome in mind, and making decisions swiftly.

It's not simply about productivity. I happily invest my energy in ways that simply bring me joy: my children, reading, interesting conversations with friends, and learning new things for fun, to name a few.

The important thing is to be intentional about where we put our energy so that we apply it to what matters most to us. Here's how:

1. *Notice your energy.* Where do you spend it? I set my phone to beep at random times during

the day as a prompt to notice how I'm spending my energy at that moment—both visibly (doing) and invisibly (thinking). When you look at life with an energy lens, you begin to see things differently. Simply doing this little energy check-in began to change my habits.

2. *Know what matters to you.* Knowing what brings value to your life—joy and productivity, for me—is essential to making smart decisions about where to invest your energy.

3. *Plan wise energy investment.* Once you know which things matter most to you, schedule as many of them into your life as possible. Put them in your calendar. Let them crowd out activities that represent energy leaks. This idea of "crowding out" works for thinking, too. Where

(continued)

INVEST YOUR ENERGY

do you want to invest your mental energy? I find that perseverating over things (or people) that annoy me is almost never a useful way to spend energy. But thinking about what I can learn from something almost always is. Let your learning mind crowd out your complaining mind.

4. *Most importantly, plan where **not** to invest your energy.* Once you begin to notice your energy, you will clearly see things you do and ways you think that are pointless energy drains. While it's surprisingly hard to stop doing something midstream, it's much less painful to not start in the first place. Think of how much easier it is *not* to turn on the television than to stop watching in the middle of a show.

Don't enter a conversation that you know will rile you up and get you nowhere.

5. *Don't spend much time thinking about it.* Optimizing your energy expenditure can become its own counterproductive energy drain. You don't have to get it right, just better than yesterday. Simply pull yourself out of one useless conversation, stop yourself from responding to one silly email, let go of one nagging thought, and you'll be a more intelligent investor of your energy.

Sometimes the solution to a problem isn't to do more. It's to do less.

Peter Bregman is the CEO of Bregman Partners, an executive coaching company that helps successful people become exceptional leaders and stellar human beings. The bestselling author of *18 Minutes* and *Leading with Emotional Courage*, his most recent book is *You Can Change Other People*.

Excerpted from "5 Steps to Investing Your Energy More Wisely," on hbr.org, March 8, 2016 (product #H02PK1).

Understand Your Tendency

When facing a goal, do you tend to get into a high-drive gear and try to remain there 24/7? Do you operate at a low-drive level most of the time, often having to scurry to the finish line at the last minute? Do you find yourself vacillating between extremes where one day you compulsively work until the wee hours of the night, and the next day you crash and do next to nothing?

Depending on your tendency, you can proceed in one of the following three ways:

- For those in the first, high-drive category, you'll need to give yourself permission to be human, to rest, and to have real downtime. Keep a close eye on whether you're going over your upper boundary of activity and headed for burnout.

- For those in the second, low-drive category, keep a close eye on whether or not you're staying above your lower bound. You want to ensure that you're doing at least the minimum before chilling out (as tempting as that may seem).

- For those in the third, fluctuating-drive category, you'll need to keep an eye on both bounds. Avoiding going over your upper bound should prevent you from falling below your lower bound the next day.

As McKeown wisely writes in his book, "Do not do more today than you can completely recover from by tomorrow."

Build In Rest and Recovery

As humans, we're designed for cycles of activity and rest. That's why we sleep at night, why weekends are an essential part of a productive workweek, and why even elite athletes can't work out every waking hour.

If you're a high-drive individual, you'll need to remain especially conscious about giving yourself planned times of rest and recovery. Since I fall toward this tendency, I make sure that my personal time isn't as jam-packed as my work time. For me, that means viewing my nonwork time not only as time to complete personal tasks, but also as time for rest. For instance, two mornings a week I don't do my normal 5:15 a.m. wakeup for swimming. Instead, I give myself time to contemplate life, read interesting articles, or simply sleep in. I also consciously take time on the weekends and evenings to connect with people without a time limit—just going with the flow and allowing things to take as long as they take.

If you operate at a low-drive level, make sure you've at least hit your lower boundary of activity before taking a break. That means that you can still take ample breaks, but only after you've made progress on a goal.

And if your drive fluctuates, you'll need to remember to have rest and recovery on the days when you feel on top of the world and like you can work 24/7 so that you don't crash the next day. That could include the basics like taking time to eat, moving from your chair by stretching or walking, and not staying up crazy late—no matter how energized you feel. Force yourself to stop when it's a reasonable time for you to go to bed so that you can begin again fresh the next day.

Give Yourself Breathing Room

To have staying power, you need to keep your work within sustainable boundaries—and you need to work at a sustainable pace. There are days when back-to-back meetings are necessary or when you need to go from task to task to task. But for most people, this strategy doesn't have long-term viability.

I encourage you, if at all possible, to have at least a few hours in a day or week where you're not in meetings. And even better, if you can block out larger chunks of time for accomplishing bigger projects, you can give yourself permission to really be immersed in the work without the pressure of a tight time window. For me, I accomplish this goal by taking Wednesday as a day free of coaching calls. That allows me to get specific projects done, such as writing this article. My whole Wednesday is blocked on a recurring basis as "Project Day" so that no one can schedule meetings with me. And I find that if you can work from home or in a private spot on days when you want to do more deep work, then it's usually easier to do so without getting interrupted.

Life isn't a sprint. It's an ongoing journey. And to stay high-performing, healthy, and happy both inside and outside of work, you need to have staying power. Look closely at how you work and follow these tips to ensure that you're working effectively, productively, and within your bounds.

ELIZABETH GRACE SAUNDERS is a time management coach and the founder of Real Life E Time Coaching & Speaking. She is the author of *How to Invest Your Time Like Money* and *Divine Time Management*. Find out more at www.RealLifeE.com.

Adapted from content posted on hbr.org, May 14, 2021
(product #H06CNV).

5

When Your Motivation Dips, Focus on Results

By Elizabeth Grace Saunders

No matter how generally motivated we are, all of us have some tasks that we don't want to do. Maybe we find them boring, pointless, draining, time-consuming, annoying, or anxiety producing. So how do you get moving in these types of situations?

Find Your Why

The first step is to recognize that getting motivated doesn't mean that you have to experience a particular feeling, like excitement or anticipation. Instead, motivation is simply one or more reasons you have for acting in a certain way. You can decide to do something without ever getting excited about it by finding a personally meaningful *why*.

For example, you could choose to do something because it will:

- Lower your anxiety

- Benefit someone who you care about

- Lead to financial gain

- Avoid a negative consequence

- Make you feel good about yourself

- Clear your mind

- Align with your values

- Reduce stress

These reasons might sound something like this in your day-to-day life:

"I don't want to do _____. But if I do _____, then I will see a significant financial payoff both now and in the future and will feel good about my choices."

"I don't want to do _____. But if I get _____ done, then it will make my boss happy and lower my anxiety every time I have a one-on-one meeting."

"I don't want to do _____. But if I make progress on _____, then I will have so much less stress next week and be prepared for _____."

Even if we never feel particularly motivated by a task, we can find a reason to move forward by looking beyond the task to the results.

Develop a Strategy

The second step for success involves coming up with a strategy for getting tasks done when you have a low to nonexistent emotional drive. Depending on the task and your work style, one or more of these strategies may help. You can consider these methods as tools in your toolbox when you've come up with a reason to take action on a task but still feel uncertain on how to complete it.

One set of action-taking methods includes involving other people in the process. This positive social pressure can provide the impetus to get something done. This could look like delegating part of the task, teaming up with someone else to complete the activity together, getting accountability, or simply being present with other people who are also working. In regard to the last point, for some of my time management coaching clients, this can look like sitting in a library where other people are also getting work done, or even having a virtual session where they work on a task while someone they know is on the other side of a video call also cranking away.

Another set of action-taking methods revolves around how you structure your approach to the work. These types of strategies, each illustrated with an example, can help you to gain momentum when you have low drive to move forward:

- Put a low-frequency activity ahead of a high-frequency activity. For example, I can't open my email until I've filed my expense report.

- Give yourself a standard time. Every Friday from 2 p.m. to 3 p.m., I have time blocked in my calendar for weekly planning, and I honor that time as sacred for that activity.

- Limit the time commitment. I need to work for 10 minutes a day on this task and then I can stop if I want to do so.

- Set the bar low. I just need to take one action step a week on this activity.

- Get it done. I want to get this entirely off my plate, so I'm setting aside a whole day to complete the task.

Pair the Unpleasant with Something Pleasant

A third set of action-taking methods involves pairing unpleasurable activities with pleasurable ones to boost your overall mood. This could involve giving yourself permission to do a more difficult task, like writing or putting together a presentation, in a location you really like, such as a cozy coffee shop or even a park if the weather is nice. You can also try layering tasks, such as listening to music or a podcast while organizing your office. Even getting a little physical activity in during the process can help. I have been known to practice speeches while going on walks. I probably look a little funny, but I get two activities done at once.

When you employ one or more of these strategies, you may not make speedy progress or perfect progress. But you can move tasks forward, slowly but surely, and get the things done that you don't naturally want to do.

ELIZABETH GRACE SAUNDERS is a time management coach and the founder of Real Life E Time Coaching & Speaking. She is the author of *How to Invest Your Time Like Money* and *Divine Time Management*. Find out more at www.RealLifeE.com.

Adapted from "How to Motivate Yourself to Do Things You Don't Want to Do," on hbr.org, December 21, 2018 (product #H04PCV).

6

Minimize Burnout by Making Compassion a Habit

By Annie McKee and Kandi Wiens

am sick to death of the ridiculous situations I have to deal with at work. The pettiness, the politics, the stupidity—it's out of control. This kind of thing stresses me out to the max."

Stress is a happiness killer. And life is just too short to be unhappy at work. But we hear this kind of thing all the time from leaders in industries as varied as financial services, education, pharmaceuticals, and health care. In our coaching and consulting, we're seeing a spike in the number of leaders who used to love their jobs but now say things like, "I'm not sure it's worth it anymore." They're burned out—emotionally exhausted and cynical—as a result of chronic and acute work stress.

Why is stress on the rise? A lot of it has to do with uncertainty in the world and constant changes in our organizations. Many people are overworking, putting in more hours than ever before. The lines between work and home have blurred or disappeared. Add to that persistent (sometimes even toxic) conflicts with bosses and coworkers that put us on guard and make us irritable. Under these circumstances, our performance and well-being suffer. Work feels like a burden. Burnout is just around the corner. And happiness at work is not even a remote possibility.

Here's the good news: Some people *don't* get burned out. They continue to thrive despite the difficult conditions in their workplace.

Why? The answer lies in part with empathy, an emotional intelligence competency packed with potent stress-taming powers. Empathy is "compassion in action." When you engage empathy, you seek to understand people's needs, desires, and point of view. You feel and express genuine concern for their well-being, and then you *act on it*.

One of our studies (Kandi's research on executive-level health-care leaders) confirms this.[1] When asked how they deal with chronic and acute work stress, 91% of the study's executives described how expressing empathy allows them to stop focusing on themselves and connect with others on a much deeper level. Other researchers agree: Expressing empathy produces physiological effects that calm us in the moment and strengthen our long-term sustainability.[2] It evokes responses in our body that arouse the (good) parasympathetic nervous system, and it reverses the effects of the stress response brought on by the (bad) sympathetic nervous system. So not only do others benefit from our empathy, but we benefit, too.

Based on our research—Annie's with leaders in global companies and Kandi's with health-care leaders—we offer a two-part strategy that can help unleash empathy and break the burnout cycle. First, you need to practice self-compassion. Then you will be ready to change some of your habitual ways of dealing with people so you—and they—can benefit from your empathy.

Practice Self-Compassion

If you really want to deal with stress, you've got to stop trying to be a hero and start caring for and about yourself. Self-compassion involves: (1) seeking to truly *understand* yourself and what you are experiencing emotionally, physically, and intellectually at work; (2) *caring* for yourself, as opposed to shutting down; and (3) *acting* to help yourself. Here are two practical ways to practice self-compassion:

- *Curb the urge to overwork.* When the pressure is on at work, we're often tempted to work more hours to "get on top of things." But overwork is a trap, not a solution. Just doing more—and more, and more, and more—rarely fixes problems, and it usually makes things worse, because we are essentially manufacturing our own stress. We shut the proverbial door on people and problems, thinking that if we can get away, we can at least do our job without getting caught up in others' drama. When nothing changes or it gets worse, we give up. This is a vicious cycle: Overwork leads to more stress, which leads to isolation, which causes us to give up, which leads to even more stress. So, instead of putting in more hours when you're stressed, find ways to renew yourself. Exercise, practice mindfulness, spend more time with loved ones, and dare we say, get more sleep?

- *Stop beating yourself up.* Stress is often the result of being too hard on ourselves when we fail or don't meet our own expectations. We forget to treat ourselves as living, breathing, feeling human beings. Instead of letting self-criticism stress you out, acknowledge how you feel, acknowledge that others would feel similarly in the same situation, and be kind and forgiving to yourself. Shifting your mindset from *threatened* to *self-compassion* will strengthen your resiliency.

Give Empathy

Taking steps toward self-compassion will prepare you emotionally to reach out to others. But let's face it: Empathy is not the norm in many workplaces. In fact, lack of empathy, even depersonalization of others, are symptoms of the emotional exhaustion that comes with burnout. Here are a few tips to make empathy part of your normal way of dealing with people at work:

- *Build friendships with people you like at work.* Most people can rattle off a dozen reasons why you shouldn't be friends with people at work. We believe just the opposite. Real connections and friendships at work matter—a lot. According to the Harvard Grant Study, one of the longest-running longitudinal studies of human development, having warm relationships is essential to health, well-being, and happiness.[3] Other research shows that caring for and feeling cared for by others lowers our blood pressure, enhances our immunity, and leads to overall better health.

- *Value people for who they really are.* The "ridiculous situations" mentioned by the leader at the beginning of this chapter are often the result of miscommunication and misunderstanding. Instead of really listening, we hear what we want to, which is misinformed by biases and stereotypes. It gets in the way of our ability to understand and connect with others. The resulting conflicts cause a lot of unnecessary stress. To prevent this, be curious about people. Ask yourself, "How can I understand where this person is coming from?" Listen with an open mind so that you gain their trust, which is good for your stress level and your ability to influence them.

- *Coach people.* According to research by Richard Boyatzis, Melvin Smith, and 'Alim Beveridge, coaching others has positive psychophysiological effects that restore the body's natural healing and growth processes and improves stamina.[4] When we care enough to invest time in developing others, we become less preoccupied with ourselves, which balances the toxic effects of stress and burnout.

- *Put your customers, clients, or patients at the center of your conversations.* If misaligned goals with coworkers is a source of your stress, try physically moving your conversations to a place where you can put other people's needs at the center. One chief medical officer who participated in Kandi's study described a time when he had an intense, stressful argument with two other physicians about the treatment plan for a terminally ill cancer patient. They were in a conference room debating and debating, with no progress on a decision. Seeing that everyone's professional conduct was declining and stress levels were rising, the CMO decided to take the conversation to the patient's room. He sat on one side of the patient's bed, holding her hand. The other two physicians sat on the opposite side of the bed, holding her other hand. They began talking again, but this time *literally* with the patient at the center of their conversation. As the CMO said, "The conversation took on a very different tone when we were able to refocus. Everyone was calm. It brought us to the same level. We were connected. It was a very effective antidote to stress."

One caution about empathy and compassion: They can be powerful forces in our fight against stress—until they aren't. Caring too much can hurt. Overextending your empathy can take a toll on your emotional resources and lead to compassion fatigue, a phenomenon that occurs when compassion becomes a burden and results in even more stress. So pay close attention to your limits and develop strategies to rein in excessive empathy if it gets out of control.

It's worth the risk, though. Once you commit to caring about yourself, you can start to care about others, and in the process, you will create resonant relationships that are both good for you and good for the people you work with.

ANNIE McKEE is a senior fellow at the University of Pennsylvania Graduate School of Education and the director of the PennCLO Executive Doctoral Program. She is the author of *How to Be Happy at Work* (Harvard Business Review Press, 2017) and a coauthor of *Primal Leadership* (Harvard Business Review Press, 2016), *Resonant Leadership* (Harvard Business Review Press, 2005) and *Becoming a Resonant Leader* (Harvard Business Review Press, 2008). KANDI WIENS is a senior fellow at the University of Pennsylvania Graduate School of Education where she is the codirector of the Penn Master's in Medical Education Program. She also teaches frequently in various Wharton Executive Education programs and in the PennCLO Executive Doctoral Program and is an executive coach and national speaker.

Notes

1. Kandi J. Wiens, "Leading Through Burnout: The Influence of Emotional Intelligence on the Ability of Executive Level Physician Leaders to Cope with Occupational Stress and Burnout" (PhD diss., University of Pennsylvania, 2016).

2. Kathryn Birnie, Michael Speca, and Linda E. Carlson, "Exploring Self-Compassion and Empathy in the Context of Mindfulness-Based Stress Reduction (MBSR)," *Stress and Health* 26 (November 2010): 359–371, https://self-compassion.org/wp-content/uploads/publications/MBSR-Exploring_self-compassion_empathy_in_the_context_of_mindfulness_based_stress_reduction.pdf; Helen Riess, "The Power of Empathy," TEDxMiddlebury, December 12, 2013, https://www.youtube.com/watch?v=baHrcC8B4WM; Richard J. Davidson, "Toward a Biology of Positive Affect and Compassion," in *Visions of Compassion: Western Scientists and Tibetan Buddhists Examine Human Nature*, ed. Richard J. Davidson and Anne Harrington (New York: Oxford University Press, 2001).

3. Robert Waldinger, "What Makes a Good Life? Lessons from the Longest Study on Happiness," TEDxBeaconStreet, November 2015, https://www.ted.com/talks/robert_waldinger_what_makes_a_good_life_lessons_from_the_longest_study_on_happiness.

4. Richard E. Boyatzis, Melvin L. Smith, and 'Alim J. Beveridge, "Coaching with Compassion: Inspiring Health, Well-Being, and Development in Organizations," *Journal of Applied Behavioral Science* 49, no. 2 (June 2013): 153–178.

Adapted from "Prevent Burnout by Making Compassion a Habit," on hbr.org, May 11, 2017 (product #H03NLJ).

7

The More You Energize Your Coworkers, the Better Everyone Performs

By Wayne Baker

How much energy do you have at work? Do you feel invigorated and engaged or down and disengaged? Either way, the reason might be your coworkers: They are infecting you with their energy, positive or negative.

We "catch" energy through our interactions with people—something called "relational energy"—and it affects our performance at work. This is what my colleagues Bradley Owens, Dana Sumpter, Kim Cameron, and I learned.[1] We were motivated to do this research because energy is a vital personal and organizational resource, but research on the sources of energy have neglected a source that everyone experiences in everyday life—our relationships with others. In a series of four empirical studies, we sought to establish relational energy as a valid scientific construct and evaluate its impact on employee engagement and job performance.

To understand how this works, think of people in your workplace who buoy you up, who lift your spirits. What do they do? What do they say? Some people are energizing because they give off positive vibes. As an employee in a large company told us about his boss, "She energized me because she loved her job and was in general a very happy person. She always came in with a smile on her face, which created a positive atmosphere." Others energize us because they create genuine connections. In conversations, for example, they devote their full attention and listen carefully.

If you have an energizing boss, chances are that you feel engaged at work. Focusing on relational energy between leaders and members of a large healthcare organization, we found that the experience of relational energy with a leader increases one's motivation at work, attention to tasks, and absorption in work activities. This translates into higher work performance. Members of this health-care company who experienced relational energy with their leaders were more engaged at work, which then led to higher productivity.

Interactions are energizing in several ways, as Rob Cross, Andrew Parker, and I learned in a series of studies of energy in organizations.[2] They include instances when we create a positive vision, when we contribute meaningfully to a conversation, when people are fully present and attentive, and when we have an interaction that gives us a sense of progress and hope.

You are a source of relational energy as well as a recipient. When you generate relational energy in the workplace, your performance goes up. Rob Cross and I discovered this in research we did on energy mapping, using organizational network analysis to reveal the network of energy in the workplace.[3] The more people you energize, the higher your work performance. This occurs because people want to be around you. You attract talent, and people are more likely to devote their discretionary time to your projects. They'll offer new ideas, information, and opportunities to you first.

The opposite is also true. If you de-energize others, people won't go out of their way to work with you or to help you. In the worst case, they might even sabotage you at work.

What can you do to increase relational energy in your workplace? Here are four actions you can take personally and as a leader.

Build high-quality connections

By definition, high-quality connections generate relational energy. Jane Dutton and Emily Heaphy suggest several ways you can grow and improve high-quality connections, such as taking on a challenge at work with a group of like-minded people.[4] In one case, two operational leaders at Kelly Services, a workforce solutions firm, created a business resource group to promote leadership development and increase employee engagement. As Dutton and Heaphy describe, the leaders focused on building high-quality connections and strengthening social capital as ways to improve the leadership pipeline.

Create energizing events

Organize and run events with an explicit focus on creating energy, not just on delivering content, products, or services. Consider how Zingerman's, a renowned community of food-related businesses in Ann Arbor, Michigan, infuses energy in its seminars and events. I often bring groups of executives to its restaurant, the Roadhouse. After dinner, CEO and cofounder Ari Weinzweig or one of his managing partners will present on a particular topic, such as visioning, open book management, or the natural laws of business. The content and delivery are fantastic and energizing themselves. But energy goes up another level when a panel of frontline staff come into the room and field questions. They can answer any question, but what matters even more is the energy they exude. They are positive, enthusiastic, and clearly love their work and the organization. The executives leave the event abuzz with energy because it's so contagious.

Use tools that promote a "giver" culture

The act of helping someone at work creates energy in the form of positive emotions—the "warm glow" of helping. Receiving help creates energy in the form of gratitude. Gratitude for help received encourages paying it forward and helping others, as Nat Bulkley and I documented in a large-scale study.[5] The Reciprocity Ring, a group-level exercise involving giving and getting help that my spouse, Cheryl Baker, CEO of Humax, created, elevates giver behaviors—and energy. In a pilot study Adam Grant and I conducted, we found that participation in the Reciprocity Ring increases positive emotions and decreases negative emotions.

Try mapping relational energy

Organizational network surveys map the invisible network behind the organizational chart—the real way people interact. Some years ago, Rob Cross and I started adding an energy question to the usual set of network questions we asked in our organizational research and consulting. Presenting each respondent with a list of names of others in the organization, we asked, "When you interact with each person, how does it affect your energy?" Responses could range from "very energizing" to "neutral" to "very de-energizing." The resulting data enabled us to draw relational energy maps of an organization. The results are quite revealing. In a large petrochemical company, for example, we found a lot of de-energizing relationships—and most of them emanated from the leaders. With this objective map, they could identify where they needed to make positive improvements. Energy maps help you target where to focus on building high-quality connections, creating energizing events, and using tools that create an energizing giver culture.

So if you feel like you have an energy crisis in your organization, the good news is that you can do something about it by focusing on relational energy—the energy we get and give in our daily interactions. Every action and word, no matter how small, matters in boosting productivity and performance.

WAYNE BAKER is the Robert P. Thome Professor of Business Administration at the University of Michigan Ross School of Business and a faculty member of the Center for Positive Organizations. His research on reciprocity, social capital, and positive organizational scholarship is available at www.waynebaker.org.

Notes

1. Bradley P. Owens et al., "Relational Energy at Work: Implications for Job Engagement and Job Performance," *Journal of Applied Psychology* 101, no. 1 (2016): 35–49.
2. Rob Cross, Wayne Baker, and Andrew Parker, "What Creates Energy in Organizations?" *MIT Sloan Management Review*, July 15, 2003.
3. "How to Energize Colleagues," *Harvard Management Update*, February 28, 2008, https://hbr.org/2008/02/how-to-energize-colleagues-1.
4. Jane E. Dutton and Emily D. Heaphy, "We Learn More When We Learn Together," hbr.org, January 12, 2016, https://hbr.org/2016/01/we-learn-more-when-we-learn-together.
5. Gretchen Gavett, "The Paying-It-Forward Payoff," hbr.org, June 30, 2014, https://hbr.org/2014/06/the-paying-it-forward-payoff.

Adapted from content posted on hbr.org, September 15, 2016 (product #H034TD).

8

How Women at the Top Can Renew Their Mental Energy

By Merete Wedell-Wedellsborg

For women with leadership ambitions, there is no shortage of advice for how to reach the top.

By learning to lean in, speak out, negotiate, delegate, and a dozen other behaviors, women everywhere are launching themselves through the glass ceilings of their organizations, landing jobs at or near the C-suite level.

But what happens *after* the promotion? While top-level jobs are tough on everyone, the transition to senior management comes with extra challenges for women. Some are psychological, pertaining to gender differences in risk-taking and self-confidence. Others are structural; in parenting, for instance, childcare and domestic duties are still disproportionately shouldered by the female partner. While these barriers affect women at all levels of the organization, they are particularly pronounced in the pressure-cooker environment at the top, putting women at a disadvantage.

Dealing with this challenge is something I am deeply familiar with. I am a certified organizational psychologist with a PhD in business economics. For more than 20 years, I have served as an executive coach to hundreds of senior women leaders, many of them working in heavily male-dominated environments such as banking, the military, and the police force. My work has given me some insights into how women leaders can improve their chances of success once they have reached the top.

At the center is managing your mental energy: how to gain it, maintain it, and not drain it. The three tactics that my female clients have used to succeed in the particular context of a top-level job are knowing your superchargers, finding a work ally, and reducing your anxiety levels.

Know Your Psychological Superchargers

Like it or not, in all but the most evolved organizations, the idea of maintaining a work-life balance at the very top is simply fictional. As Alexandra, a U.S. hedge fund partner, told me: "If you want balance, go be a yoga nidra instructor." Another top management team I worked with had the motto "Deliver or Die"; there was little doubt as to where "me time" belonged in that particular team's list of priorities. Given this brutal reality, combined with the extra domestic burdens imposed on many women, how do female top leaders manage to recharge their batteries?

Part of the answer lies in realizing that not all sources of energy are equal. Specifically, some activities are what I call "psychological superchargers"—that is, activities that yield a disproportionately bigger energy boost than others. The nature of these superchargers varies from person to person—I'll share some examples shortly—but consistently, the most successful women I've worked with figured out what theirs were and made sure to tap into them regularly.

In looking for your own superchargers, keep two things in mind: First, set aside culturally mandated ideas about what women are supposed or not supposed to gain energy from (spoiler alert: spending time with kids is not always a net contributor to your mental reserves), and look instead to your quirkier sides. One leader I worked with got her mental boost from filling out a type of paint-by-numbers mandala drawing; for her, it was an almost meditative activity. Another leader found it hugely energizing to browse executive education programs she might sign up for, as if perusing intellectual holiday destinations. As she told me, "I get my fix from the way it makes the world feel bigger." A third one found energy in literature and in following new trends in a totally different field.

Second, indulge your inner hedonist. On the personality tests I use, many of the female leaders I coach score very low on hedonism-related measures. They are highly conscientious people, a trait that served to get them into the top job, but they also have a tendency to forget having fun and enjoying life. Perhaps for that reason, superchargers not uncommonly involve a bit of lavish spending. Senior leadership positions tend to come with bigger paychecks, and while your instinct might be to save the money, don't forget that occasional self-indulgent spending can be a good investment, too.

Find a Work Ally

Your personal life, of course, is not the only source of energy; under the right conditions, your work can also contribute to your mental reserves. This is especially true if your team is characterized by what Harvard Business School's Amy Edmondson calls psychological safety; that is, the sense that your teammates are on your side, and that it's safe to make mistakes or say something stupid within the group.[1]

The problem is, those conditions are generally not present at the top. Senior leadership teams are often political, and failures typically have much larger consequences. And while it is possible to build a real sense of team spirit at the top with time and effort, new team members can rarely count on partaking in it before they've proven themselves. What, then, can be done to create a psychological work environment that helps maintain your energy?

The answer, I've found, is to abandon the idea that your team as a whole can serve as a safe place. Instead, concentrate on gaining a single close ally—that is, a person in your team that you feel free to discuss things with behind the scenes and use as an outlet for the inevitable frustrations that come with the job. The successful senior-level women I've worked with can immediately answer the question, "Who can you speak freely to?"—and they are deliberate about cultivating these relationships, using them to maintain their energy as part of the day-to-day.

With luck, you may have an ally on the team already. But if you don't, there are ways you can speed up the process of creating such a relationship. First, don't necessarily focus on gender. It may feel natural to try to ally yourself with another woman (if the team has one). But what I've found to be more important than gender is shared values: that the other person is someone you can relate to on a deeper level, and someone you can feel free to share a laugh with. Alliances of this nature have strong parallels to friendships—some of my clients refer to them as "work marriages"—and their formation often transcends more superficial commonalities.

Second, make your own particular passions known. Alexandra, the hedge fund partner, had colleagues who were obsessed with American football, but as she told me: "I never talk about sports. It doesn't interest me." Instead, she regularly brought up the things she cared about and sought out the individuals who responded to those things, building her relationships based on authentic commonalities.

Finally, create opportunities to talk to people one-on-one, outside of the usual work setting. For some, this means sharing a car ride to an off-site or making sure you get a seat next to each other on a long flight. Daily routines can help, too: Some of my clients have built alliances through exercising together or carpooling on their way to or from work, using that time to discuss new ideas or figuring out how to cope with the political game around them. There is something about such "offstage" periods that promotes opening up and sets the stage for creating stronger bonds.

Overcome Anxiety by Channeling Your Values

Risk-taking is part and parcel of corporate careers, and few people, men or women, enter the top ranks of the organization without having made a bold gamble or two along the way. But at the top, the nature of risk-taking changes significantly. There is a lot more at stake; there are much larger degrees of uncertainty around the choices you'll have to make; and decisions might require you to stand alone, going against an otherwise unified group of people with more seniority in the role.

In my experience, women struggle with this shift a lot more than men, to the point where anxiety becomes an overriding emotion in their new role. This creates a double handicap. As an always-on background emotion, anxiety becomes a major energy leech, constantly siphoning off your mental surplus.

At the same time, when your anxiety level is high, it is difficult to take chances with new approaches, or even to see the situation with clear eyes. So, how should female leaders find the daily courage to step up to the plate, make tough choices, or stand alone on an issue—all while not allowing the pressure to drain away their energy?

It's all rooted in your larger motivation: Do you focus on your career, aiming to maintain or even improve your position or political standing in the group? Or do you focus more on making a difference? Paradoxically, I find that women who focus on their career as their main goal are less likely to be truly impactful as a leader. When your biggest aim is to avoid visible failures, the temptation to play it safe can lead to a career dominated by perpetual anxiety and by a fatal tendency to shy away from the tough career-defining calls.

In comparison, the successful top-level women I've coached were certainly mindful of their careers. But they didn't see it as an end goal. Rather, they saw it as a tool to create results, changes, and breakthroughs around things they really cared about. Their focus on doing what's right created a mental bulwark against the more extreme degrees of anxiety, allowing them to keep calm under pressure and save their energy for where it was most needed.

For that reason, ask yourself: What can I vouch for? The ability to have the courage of your convictions is essential, as is having the nerve to follow a path—not because it is the easiest and most pleasant way to go, but because it represents the right solution when things are chaotic and difficult. Even in the stormiest sea, there is a calm that comes with staying true to your convictions.

Jointly, the three tactics I have outlined here can make a real difference in terms of managing your energy and succeeding at the top. And in more ways than one, doing so is crucial, because a lot hangs in the balance. Unfairly or not, the women who now enter top management face the added burden of showing that they can perform as well or better than their male peers. It's not enough to shatter the glass ceiling. We need to focus on how more women can reach the top—*and* how they can perform once they have arrived.

MERETE WEDELL-WEDELLSBORG runs her own business psychology practice with clients in the financial, pharmaceutical, and defense sectors, as well as family offices. Merete holds a PhD in business economics from Copenhagen Business School and an MA in psychology from the University of Copenhagen (clinical psychology). She is the author of *Battle Mind: How to Navigate in Chaos and Perform Under Pressure*.

Note

1. Amy Edmondson, "Psychological Safety and Learning Behavior in Work Teams," *Administrative Science Quarterly* 44, no. 2 (1999): 350–383.

Adapted from content posted on hbr.org, April 16, 2018 (product #H04A4R).

9

Five Ways to Focus Your Energy During a Work Crunch

By Amy Jen Su

Work invariably ebbs and flows, cycling between steady states, where we feel more in control of the pace and workload, and peak periods, where the work crunch hits us hard. Unexpected setbacks, project sprints, or even vacations and holidays can create mayhem and tension. Maintaining focus and managing energy levels become critical as tasks pile onto an already full load. When you're in your next work crunch, there are a few things you can do to focus and manage your energy more productively.

Accept the situation

When an acute period hits, it's easy to resist the fact that it's happening. We wish for things to be like they were last month, or we long for the pace we had during vacation. By not being present in the here and now, we drain our energy by ruminating on the situation. In fact, physicists define resistance as "the degree to which a substance or device opposes the passage of an electrical current, causing energy dissipation." In the case of a work crunch, the more you oppose what's happening, the more energy you lose. Acceptance does not mean giving in.[1] On the contrary, it means acknowledging the reality of the situation with awareness so that you can take clear action.

Observe and label your underlying emotions

Acceptance is particularly difficult given the underlying emotions that an acute work crunch can bring.

Negative thoughts such as *I'm not going to do a good job, I don't know if I'll be able to get it all done*, or *I feel like I'm dropping the ball at both home and work* often predominate. David Rock, director of the Neuro-Leadership Institute, suggests in his book *Your Brain at Work* that, rather than suppressing or denying an emotion, an effective cognitive technique is labeling, whereby you take a situation and put a label on your emotions. "The most successful executives have developed an ability to be in a state of high limbic system arousal and still remain calm," Rock says. "Partly, this is their ability to label emotion states."

The next time you are in a tough work crunch, or you're experiencing a setback at work, take Rock's advice to step back, observe your thinking and emotional state, and assign a word to what's happening, such as "pressure," "guilt," or "worry." By using just one or two words, Rock's research shows, you can reduce the arousal of the limbic brain's fight-or-flight system and instead activate the prefrontal cortex, which is responsible for our executive functioning skills.

Preserve your sense of choice and agency

Accepting the situation and labeling our emotions can help to reduce the anxiety that comes with a work crunch. This is critical, because, as research out of the University of Pittsburgh shows, anxiety directly impacts our cognitive functioning, especially those areas responsible for making sound decisions.[2] Don't fall into a victim mentality, believing there are no choices or that you don't have control. Instead, bring greater vigilance to assessing your priorities, making tough trade-offs, and incorporating self-care where you can. For example, ask yourself:

- What are the one to two things that are mission critical today?

- What is something I can do to recharge my battery (get to bed early one night this week, listen

to my favorite music while working, or catch a
nap on a plane)?

- Who or what will I have to say no to during
  this time?

Communicate with your colleagues
and loved ones

Other people can be a real energy drain—or gain—
during work crunches and setbacks. Pause and consider how you can renegotiate deadlines, set tighter
boundaries, or ask for more support during this time:

- *Renegotiate deadlines.* Loop back with colleagues to ensure that you understand when
  the other person really needs something and is
  going to review it. In other cases, if you antici-
  pate not being able to meet a deadline, be sure
  to inform your colleagues of the new timing
  or renegotiate it. Keep your integrity by doing

what you say you're going to do and being up front about when you need to shift gears.

- *Set tighter boundaries.* Our boundaries and guardrails need to be different during work crunches or acute periods. Let others, both professionally and personally, know when you'll be available or not so they are aware of your more limited schedule.

- *Ask for help and support.* Many of us pride ourselves on not bothering others and being self-reliant. These are great qualities, but there are times when we need to ask for help. Ask your loved ones for more help on the home front. Share the weight of the accountability for projects with your colleagues by delegating or teaming up, versus doing it all on your own.

Practice self-compassion

Probably the toughest thing of all during a work crunch or setback is how easy it is to beat yourself up, especially when you aren't hitting your high standards for work or time at home. Annie McKee, author of *How to Be Happy at Work* and coauthor of several books on emotional intelligence, says this about self-compassion: "If you really want to deal with stress, you've got to stop trying to be a hero and start caring for and about yourself."

To be truly self-compassionate, especially during an acute period of work stress, accept the situation by acknowledging it with awareness and compassion, observe and label your emotions (don't suppress or deny them), preserve your sense of choice and agency, communicate with your colleagues and loved ones, and ask for help when you need it. By taking these actions, you'll move through your next crunch with greater ease and peace.

AMY JEN SU is a cofounder and managing partner of Paravis Partners, a premier executive coaching and leadership development firm. For the past two decades, she has coached CEOs, executives, and rising stars in organizations. She is the author of *The Leader You Want to Be* (Harvard Business Review Press, 2019) and coauthor of *Own the Room* (Harvard Business Review Press, 2013) with Muriel Maignan Wilkins.

Notes

1. Steve Taylor, "How Acceptance Can Transform Your Life: The Four Stages of Acceptance," *Psychology Today*, August 19, 2015, https://www.psychologytoday.com/us/blog/out-the-darkness/201508/how-acceptance-can-transform -your-life.
2. Christopher Bergland, "How Does Anxiety Short Circuit the Decision-Making Process?" *Psychology Today*, March 17, 2016, https://www.psychologytoday.com/us/blog/the-athletes-way/201603/how-does-anxiety-short -circuit-the-decision-making-process.

Adapted from content posted on hbr.org, September 22, 2017 (product #H03WMD).

10

Resilience Is About How You Recharge, Not How You Endure

By Shawn Achor and Michelle Gielan

As frequent travelers and parents of a 2-year-old, we sometimes fantasize about how much work we can do when one of us gets on a plane, undistracted by phones, friends, and *Finding Nemo*. We race to get all our groundwork done: packing, going through security, doing a last-minute work call, calling each other, then boarding the plane. Then, when we try to have that amazing work session in flight, we get nothing done. Even worse, after refreshing our email or reading the same studies over and over, we are too exhausted when we land to soldier on with the emails that have inevitably piled up.

Why should flying deplete us? We're just sitting there doing nothing. Why can't we be tougher—more resilient and determined in our work—so we can accomplish all of the goals we set for ourselves? Based on our current research, we have come to realize that the problem is not our hectic schedule or the plane travel itself; the problem comes from a misunderstanding of what it means to be resilient, and the resulting impact of overworking.

We often take a militaristic, "tough" approach to resilience and grit. We imagine a soldier slogging through the mud, a boxer going one more round, or a football player picking himself up off the turf for one more play. We believe that the longer we tough it out, the tougher we are, and therefore the more successful we will be. However, this entire conception is scientifically inaccurate.

The very lack of a recovery period is dramatically holding back our collective ability to be resilient and successful. Research has found that there is a direct correlation between lack of recovery and increased incidence of health and safety problems.[1] And lack of recovery—whether by disrupting sleep with thoughts of work or having continuous cognitive arousal by watching our phones—is costing our companies $62 billion a year (that's billion, not million) in lost productivity.[2]

And just because work stops doesn't mean we're recovering. We "stop" work sometimes at 5 p.m., but then we spend the night wrestling with solutions to work problems, talking about our work over dinner, and falling asleep thinking about how much work we'll do tomorrow. In one study, researchers from Norway found that 7.8% of Norwegians have become workaholics.[3] The scientists cite a definition of "workaholism" as "being overly concerned about work, driven by an uncontrollable work motivation, and investing so much time and effort to work that it impairs other important life areas."[4]

We believe that the number of people who fit that definition includes the majority of American workers, which prompted us to begin a study of workaholism in the U.S. Our study will use a large corporate data set from a major medical company to examine how technology extends our working hours and thus interferes with necessary cognitive recovery, resulting in huge health-care costs and turnover costs for employers.

The misconception of resilience is often bred from an early age. Parents trying to teach their children resilience might celebrate a high school student staying up until 3 a.m. to finish a science fair project. What a distortion of resilience! A resilient child is a well-rested one. When an exhausted student goes to school, they risk hurting everyone on the road with their impaired driving; they don't have the cognitive resources to do well on their English test; they have lower self-control with their friends; and at home, they are moody with their parents. Overwork and exhaustion are the opposite of resilience. And the bad habits we learn when we're young only magnify when we hit the workforce.

In *The Sleep Revolution*, Arianna Huffington wrote, "We sacrifice sleep in the name of productivity, but ironically our loss of sleep, despite the extra hours we spend at work, adds up to 11 days of lost productivity per year per worker, or about $2,280."[5]

The key to resilience is trying really hard, then stopping, recovering, and then trying again. This conclusion is based on biology. Homeostasis is a fundamental biological concept describing the ability of the brain to continuously restore and sustain well-being.[6] Positive neuroscientist Brent Furl from Texas A&M University coined the term "homeostatic value" to describe the value that certain actions have for creating equilibrium, and thus well-being, in the body. When the body is out of alignment from overworking, we waste a vast amount of mental and physical resources trying to return to balance before we can move forward.

As Jim Loehr and Tony Schwartz have written, if you have too much time in the performance zone, you need more time in the recovery zone, otherwise you risk burnout.[7] Mustering your resources to "try hard" requires burning energy in order to overcome your currently low arousal level. This is called "up-regulation." It also exacerbates exhaustion. The more imbalanced we become due to overworking, the more value there is in activities that allow us to return to a state of balance. The value of a recovery period rises in proportion to the amount of work required of us.

So how do we recover and build resilience? Most people assume that if you stop doing a task like answering emails or writing a paper, your brain will naturally recover, such that when you start again later in the day or the next morning, you'll have your energy back. But surely everyone reading this has had times when you lie in bed for hours, unable to fall asleep because your brain is thinking about work. If you lie in bed for eight hours, you may have rested, but you can still feel exhausted the next day. That's because rest and recovery are not the same thing. Stopping does not equal recovering.

If you're trying to build resilience at work, you need adequate internal and external recovery periods. As researchers Zijlstra, Cropley, and Rydstedt explain: "Internal recovery refers to the shorter periods of relaxation that take place within the frames of the workday or the work setting in the form of short scheduled or unscheduled breaks, by shifting attention or changing to other work tasks when the mental or physical resources required for the initial task are temporarily depleted or exhausted. External recovery refers to actions that take place outside of work—for example, in the free time between the workdays, and during weekends, holidays or vacations."[8] If after work you lie around on your bed and get riled up by political commentary on your phone or get stressed thinking about deciding how to renovate your home, your brain has not received a break from high mental arousal states. Our brains need a rest as much as our bodies do.

If you really want to build resilience, you can start by strategically stopping. Give yourself the resources to be tough by creating internal and external recovery periods. In *The Future of Happiness*, based on her work at Yale School of Management, Amy Blankson describes how to strategically stop during the day by using technology to control overworking. She suggests downloading the Instant or Moment apps to see how many times you turn on your phone each day. The average person turns on their phone 150 times every day. If every distraction took only one minute (which would be seriously optimistic), that would account for two-and-a-half hours of every day.

You can use apps like Offtime or Unplugged to create tech-free zones by strategically scheduling automatic airplane modes. In addition, you can take a cognitive break every 90 minutes to recharge your batteries. Try to not have lunch at your desk, but instead spend time outside or with your friends—not talking about work. Take all of your paid time off, which not only gives you recovery periods but raises your productivity and likelihood of promotion.

As for us, we've started using our plane time as a work-free zone, and thus time to dip into the recovery phase. The results have been fantastic. We are usually tired already by the time we get on a plane, and the cramped space and spotty internet connection make work more challenging. Now, instead of swimming upstream, we relax, meditate, sleep, watch movies, journal, or listen to entertaining podcasts. And when we get off the plane, instead of being depleted, we feel rejuvenated and ready to return to the performance zone.

SHAWN ACHOR is the *New York Times* bestselling author of *Big Potential*, *The Happiness Advantage*, and *Before Happiness*. He is the chief experience officer for BetterUp. MICHELLE GIELAN, a national CBS News anchor turned UPenn positive psychology researcher, is the bestselling author of *Broadcasting Happiness*.

Notes

1. Judith K. Sluiter, "The Influence of Work Characteristics on the Need for Recovery and Experienced Health: A

Study on Coach Drivers," *Ergonomics* 42, no. 4 (1999), https://doi.org/10.1080/001401399185487.

2. American Academy of Sleep Medicine, "Insomnia Costing US Workforce $63.2 Billion a Year in Lost Productivity, Study Shows," *Science Daily*, September 2, 2011, https://www.sciencedaily.com/releases/2011/09/110901093653.htm.

3. Cecilie Schou Andreassen et al., "The Relationships Between Workaholism and Symptoms of Psychiatric Disorders: A Large-Scale Cross-Sectional Study," *PLOS ONE* 11, no. 5 (2016): e0152978, https://doi.org/10.1371/journal.pone.0152978.

4. Cecilie Schou Andreassen, Jørn Hetland, and Ståle Pallesen, "Psychometric Assessment of Workaholism Measures," *Journal of Managerial Psychology*, January 1, 2014, https://www.emerald.com/insight/content/doi/10.1108/JMP-05-2013-0143/full/html.

5. Arianna Huffington, *The Sleep Revolution: Transforming Your Life, One Night at a Time* (New York: Harmony, 2016).

6. "What Is Homeostasis? Emeritus Professor Kelvin Rodolfo of the University of Illinois at Chicago's Department of Earth and Environmental Sciences Provides This Answer," *Scientific American*, January 3, 2000, https://www.scientificamerican.com/article/what-is-homeostasis/.

7. Jim Loehr and Tony Schwartz, *The Power of Full Engagement: Managing Energy, Not Time, Is the Key to High*

Performance and Personal Renewal (New York: Free Press, 2003).

8. Fred R. H. Zijlstra, Mark Cropley, and Leif W. Rydstedt, "From Recovery to Regulation: An Attempt to Reconceptualize 'Recovery from Work,'" *Stress Health* 30, no. 3 (August 2014): 244–252.

Adapted from content posted on hbr.org, June 24, 2016 (product #H02Z3O).

11

What You Don't Know About Motivation

By Susan Fowler

At some point in their careers, most leaders have either consciously—or, more likely, unwittingly—based (or justified) their approach to motivation on Maslow's hierarchy of needs. Maslow's idea that people are motivated by satisfying lower-level needs, such as food, water, shelter, and security, before they can move on to being motivated by higher-level needs, such as self-actualization, is the most well-known motivation theory in the world.[1] There is nothing wrong with helping people satisfy what Maslow characterized as lower-level needs. Improvements in workplace conditions and safety should be applauded as the right thing to do. Seeing that people have enough food and water to meet their biological needs is the humane thing to do. Getting people off the streets into healthy environments is the decent thing to do. But the truth is, individuals can experience higher-level motivation anytime and anywhere.

Despite the popularity of Maslow's hierarchy, there is not much recent data to support it. Contemporary scientists—specifically Dr. Edward Deci—hundreds of self-determination theory researchers, and thousands of studies instead point to three universal psychological needs. If you really want to take advantage of this new science—rather than focusing on a pyramid of needs—you should focus on *autonomy*, *relatedness*, and *competence*.

Autonomy is people's need to perceive that they have choices, that what they are doing is of their own volition, and that they are the source of their own actions. The way leaders frame information and situations either promotes the likelihood that a person will perceive autonomy or undermines it. To promote autonomy:

- Frame goals and timelines as essential information to ensure a person's success, rather than as dictates or ways to hold people accountable.

- Refrain from incentivizing people through competitions and games. Few people have learned the skill of shifting the reason why they're competing from an external one (winning a prize or gaining status) to a higher-quality one (an opportunity to fulfill a meaningful goal).

- Don't apply pressure to perform. Sustained peak performance is a result of people acting because they *choose* to—not because they feel they *have* to.

Relatedness is people's need to care about and be cared for by others, to feel connected to others without concerns about ulterior motives, and to feel that they are contributing to something greater than themselves. Leaders have a great opportunity to help people derive meaning from their work. To deepen relatedness:

- Validate the exploration of feelings in the workplace. Be willing to ask people how they feel about an assigned project or goal and listen to their response. All behavior may not be acceptable, but all feelings are worth exploring.

- Take time to facilitate the development of people's values at work—then help them align those values with their goals. It is impossible to link work to values if individuals don't know what their values are.

- Connect people's work to a noble purpose.

Competence is people's need to feel effective at meeting everyday challenges and opportunities, demonstrating skill over time, and feeling a sense of growth and flourishing. Leaders can rekindle people's desire to grow and learn. To develop people's competence:

- Make resources available for learning. What message does it send about values for learning and developing competence when training budgets are the first casualty of economic cutbacks?

- Set learning goals—not just the traditional results-oriented and outcome goals.

- At the end of each day, instead of asking, "What did you achieve today?" ask, "What did you learn today? How did you grow today in ways that will help you and others tomorrow?"

Unlike Maslow's needs, these three basic needs are not hierarchical or sequential. They are foundational to all human beings and our ability to flourish.[2]

The exciting message to leaders is that when the three basic psychological needs are satisfied in the workplace, people experience the day-to-day high-quality motivation that fuels employee work passion—and all the inherent benefits that come from actively engaged individuals at work. Taking advantage of the science requires shifting your leadership focus from "What can I give people to motivate them?" to "How can I facilitate people's satisfaction of autonomy, relatedness, and competence?"

Leaders have opportunities every day to integrate these motivational practices. For example, a leader I coach was about to launch a companywide message to announce mandatory training on green solutions compliance. Ironically, his well-intentioned message dictated people's actions—undermining people's sense of autonomy and probably guaranteeing their defiance rather than compliance. His message didn't provide a values-based rationale or ask individuals to consider how their own values might be aligned to the initiative. After reconsidering his approach, he created this message embedded with ways for people to experience autonomy, relatedness, and competence:

There are three ways you can share our commitment for implementing green solutions as an essential part of our Corporate Social Responsibility initiative.

- *Join others who are passionate about reducing their carbon footprint for a fun and interactive training session on November 15.* (Relatedness)

- *Read the attached manifesto and take a quick quiz to see what you learned by November 18.* (Competence)

- *Send us your story about what you are doing at work to be environmentally responsible by November 14.* (Autonomy, competence, and relatedness)

You can choose any or all three options (Auton-omy). Let us know your preference(s) by email (Autonomy) by October 31 or stop by our table at the all-company Halloween party (Relatedness). If you choose to opt out of all three choices (Auton-omy), please tell us what we can do to appeal more directly to your values around corporate social responsibility (Relatedness).

Don't underestimate your people's capacity— indeed, their longing—to experience high-quality motivation at work anytime and anywhere.

SUSAN FOWLER is the president of Mojo Moments, Inc., and the author of the bestselling *Why Motivating People Doesn't Work . . . and What Does.*

Notes

1. Kendra Cherry, "Maslow's Hierarchy of Needs," *Very Well Mind*, January 26, 2022, https://www.verywellmind.com/ what-is-maslows-hierarchy-of-needs-4136760.

2. Edward L. Deci and Richard M. Ryan, "The Importance of Universal Psychological Needs for Understanding Motivation in the Workplace," *The Oxford Handbook of Work Engagement, Motivation, and Self-Determination Theory*, ed. Marylène Gagné, doi: 10.1093/oxfordhb/9780199794911.013.003.

Adapted from "What Maslow's Hierarchy Won't Tell You About Motivation," on hbr.org, November 26, 2014 (product #H012BN).

12

Why People Lose Motivation—and What Managers Can Do to Help

By Dan Cable

At some point, every leader has dealt with a person—or, worse, a group of people—who has lost motivation. It's frustrating, isn't it? As much as we've been there ourselves, sometimes it's hard to sympathize with others who are disengaged from work and are unproductive as a result. Sometimes, we view their unhappiness as a bug in their mental makeup—and, therefore, we think they should be able to suck it up and snap out of it.

Although it's easy to fall into this mindset as a leader, this type of thinking is counterproductive, and it ignores the underlying reasons why people lose their passion for what they do (or never find it to begin with).

In order to get at the crux of the problem, it's crucial to understand that as humans we want to feel motivated and to find meaning in the things that we do. It's part of our biology. In fact, there's a part of our brains called the seeking system that creates the natural impulses to learn new skills and take on challenging but meaningful tasks.[1] When we follow these urges, we receive a jolt of dopamine—a neurotransmitter linked to motivation and pleasure—which makes us want to engage in these activities even more.[2] And, when our seeking systems are activated, we feel more motivated, purposeful, and zestful.[3] We feel more alive.

Exploring, experimenting, learning—this is the way we're supposed to live and work. The problem is, too many workers aren't able to partake in these activities because the way our organizations are run is preventing them from doing so.

Take Tom, a website developer whom I met on a consulting assignment at an accounting firm. When Tom was hired, fresh out of college, he was excited because he had been told that there were opportunities for learning and growth. But the honeymoon didn't last long. "I soon found out my supervisor had no time or patience for experimenting," he told me. "He was more concerned with protocol than personal development. It's like he's afraid of me trying new things because it might not go exactly as planned. It doesn't leave me much room for learning."

At first, Tom wasn't deterred. He worked to improve some processes and tried to inject some personality into his work. But since Tom's boss was under pressure to meet a number of website metrics, she didn't have the flexibility to implement his ideas. As the weeks turned into months, Tom's work became routine and boring, and he shut off as a result.

We shouldn't blame Tom for his reaction, because he reacted the way we're all *designed* to react.

Shutting down is our body's way of telling us that we were meant to do better things. To keep exploring and learning. This is our biology; it is a part of our adaptive unconscious to know that our human potential is being wasted.

The key for leaders is to find ways to activate employees' seeking systems. But how do you do it? If you're like Tom's boss, there are likely organizational roadblocks in the way, many of which are probably beyond your control. It's often impossible to ignore performance metrics or overcome policies and bureaucratic red tape.

Despite these difficulties, it is possible for leaders to activate their employees' seeking systems without a large overhaul to organizationwide policies and culture. And, in my experience working with leaders across the globe, you can reach business objectives while improving the lives of employees. There are three small but consequential nudges that trigger employees' seeking systems: encourage them to play to their strengths, create opportunities to experiment, and help them personalize the purpose of the work.

Self-Expression

Philosophers have been telling us for millennia that people have an innate drive to show others who they really are, yet somehow organizational life often runs afoul of the human desire for self-expression. Even now, when we extol the virtues of creativity and innovation, we still see bureaucratic job titles, inflexible roles, and standardized evaluation systems that generate anxiety instead of excitement and self-expression.

None of us wants to just perform preprogrammed behaviors again and again. We have a deep desire to use our unique skills and perspectives to make our own decisions about how to help our teams succeed. When people are prompted to think about their best traits, their seeking systems are activated. Research shows that when people identify and use their unique strengths, they feel more alive.

Leaders can help employees be their best selves without changing the frames of their jobs. For example, in a study I conducted with colleagues, we found that asking new hires to write down and share stories about times they were at their best made them feel more comfortable about being themselves around coworkers, and that their unique strengths were valued.[4] Results showed that newcomers onboarded this way made customers happier and were much less likely to quit in the future.

Employees want to be valued for the unique skills and perspectives they bring to the table, and the more you can reinforce this and remind them of their role in the company at large, the better. And it doesn't take much. At both Make-A-Wish Foundation and Novant Health, for example, leaders encouraged employees to create their own job titles, a move that prompted people to highlight their unique contributions to their teams.

Experimentation

A second way to activate people's seeking systems is to create an experimental safe zone that includes play and supportive social bonding. Play not only stimulates the seeking system but also pushes back anxiety and fear.

Positive emotions are important in their own right, of course. But it's not just that play feels good. Experimental safe zones create intrinsic motivations, which are much more powerful than extrinsic motivations because they unleash creativity. Firms are more agile when they encourage employees to think up new approaches and try them out, and then get feedback about how the environment responded to their ideas.

The research is clear that framing change and innovation as a chance to experiment and learn is better than framing them as a performance situation, which makes people anxious, risk-averse, and less willing to persist through difficulty.[5] For example, employees in a white-goods manufacturing plant in Italy learned about lean manufacturing by playing with Legos rather than cooktops. They then experimented with transforming their own production line using the new techniques. In two weeks, the production team made lean manufacturing their own, reducing internal defects by 30% and improving productivity by 25%.

Purpose

The feeling of purpose doesn't come only from curing diseases and improving the world. The feeling of purpose also ignites when we can see the cause and effect between our inputs and our team's progress. For example, a sense of purpose soars when we can offer insights to our team about the environment and what might work better. Likewise, we feel a sense of purpose when we can experience firsthand how our unique contributions help other people and allow the team to progress.

For example, when leaders brought scholarship students into a call center to thank the fundraisers for the money they raised, the fundraisers became more persistent and made a lot more calls on their shifts. And, because they were more personally connected to the reasons for their work, each call was substantially more effective; they raised an average of $9,704.58 versus $2,459.44 for fundraisers who did not talk to a scholarship student.[6]

Keep in mind that instilling a sense of purpose doesn't work when it is a one-off. It can't just be a speech by senior leaders who speak during town hall meetings about why their products help customers.

Purpose works best when employees get to interact directly with the people they are affecting with their work. For example, employees at Microsoft are encouraged to spend time with clients, understanding their problems and issues firsthand. One account manager spent a week on the street with police officers, for example, trying to understand when and where remote data could help them. Another account manager spent two days in a hospital to understand what it would really mean to become paperless.

It doesn't take much to light up our seeking systems. For leaders, the upshot is the potential already flowing right under the surface. And it doesn't take charm or motivational speeches to tap into that energy—all it takes is a concerted effort to infuse self-expression, experimentation, and personalized purpose into all that we do.

DAN CABLE is a professor of organizational behavior at London Business School. His book *Exceptional* helps you build a personal highlight reel to unlock your potential, and his book *Alive at Work* helps you understand the neuroscience of why people love what they do.

Notes

1. Jaak Panksepp, *Affective Neuroscience: The Foundations of Human and Animal Emotions* (New York: Oxford University Press, 2004).
2. M. Koepp et al., "Evidence for Striatal Dopamine Release During a Video Game," *Nature* 393 (1998): 266–268, https://doi.org/10.1038/30498.
3. Carroll E. Izard, "Basic Emotions, Natural Kinds, Emotion Schemas, and a New Paradigm," *Perspectives on Psychological Science* 2, no. 3 (September 2007): 260–280, https://doi.org/10.1111/j.1745-6916.2007.00044.x.
4. Dan Cable, Francesca Gino, and Bradley Staats, "The Powerful Way Onboarding Can Encourage Authenticity," hbr.org, November 26, 2015, https://hbr.org/2015/11/the-powerful-way-onboarding-can-encourage-authenticity.
5. Amy C. Edmondson, "Framing for Learning: Lessons in Successful Technology Implementation," in *Fundamentals of Organization Development*, ed. David Coghlan and Abraham B. Shani, IV121, SAGE Library in Business and Management (London: Sage Publications Ltd., 2010), https://dx.doi.org/10.4135/9781446261774.n64.

6. Adam M. Grant, "The Significance of Task Significance: Job Performance Effects, Relational Mechanisms, and Boundary Conditions," *Journal of Applied Psychology* 93, no. 1 (2008): 108–124.

Adapted from content posted on hbr.org, March 12, 2018 (product #H047IC).

Index

How to be human at work.

HBR's Emotional Intelligence Series features smart, essential reading on the human side of professional life from the pages of *Harvard Business Review*. Each book in the series offers uplifting stories, practical advice, and research from leading experts on how to tend to our emotional well-being at work.

Harvard Business Review Emotional Intelligence Series

Available in paperback or ebook format. The specially priced six-volume set includes:

- Mindfulness
- Resilience
- Influence and Persuasion

- Authentic Leadership
- Happiness
- Empathy